NAVARASAM

NAVARASAM

Mona Aiyar

PAPER TOWNS
PUBLISHERS

PAPER TOWNS
PUBLISHERS

First published by
Papertowns Publishers
72, Vishwanath Dham Colony,
Niwaru Road, Jhotwara,
Jaipur, 302012

Navarasam

ISBN Print Book - 978-93-87131-78-1

"To Amma – for discovering the rhyme in my babble"

Acknowledgements

The poems in this book would have remained scattered on my blogs, or hidden in the pages of my diaries, had it not been for the constant nudges from my best friend, Shreyas Vaidya, to get them published. I can't thank him enough for making me do this!

A big thank you to my family – amma (Sunita Venkatesh), papa (Venkatesh Narayan), Neha (Dr. Neha Venkatesh) and Naren (Dr. Naren Ramachandran) for being my first readers, and making me believe in myself and my writing. A special mention to my paati (granny), Kalyani Aiyar, whose thirst for knowledge always inspired me to read, write and keep getting better.

I would like to extend my heartfelt gratitude to Narendra Singh, Aditi Shah (for her wonderful designing) and the entire team of Papertowns Publishing for helping me put this book together. A big shout-out to my friend, Shantanu Nadkar, for supporting me wholeheartedly through the publishing process.

Lastly, I am truly grateful to all my friends and my readers out there, for reading and appreciating my work and for keeping the poet in me alive!

Contents

Section 1: Shringaram

Section 2: Karunam

Section 3: Hasyam

Section 4: Raudram

Section 5: Bibhatsam

Section 6: Bhayanakam

Section 7: Veeram

Section 8: Adbhutam

Section 9: Shantham

Shringaram

(Poems of love, beauty & longing)

Hey, you!

Hey, you,
Your smile's a charm,
Or black magic maybe,
Drawn to you,
Like a magnet to iron,
Your steely arms,
If only you could clasp me in them,
I would simply collapse,
And drown in the pool of your eyes,
Run my fingers through,
That unkempt hair,
Feel your breath on my shoulder,
And melt away,
What is this spell you've cast on me,
That's making me lose my mind,
Thinking about you,
While you've no clue,
Hey, you!

Sweet tender love

Her sweet breath on his neck,
She gasps, her chest heaving up and down,
His one-day stubble against her face,
And there appears an instant frown,
He caresses her trembling body,
As she melts into his arms,
Their heavy breathing fills the room,
Which is, otherwise, so calm,
Their parched lips meet, slowly, tenderly,
In a sweet embrace,
And they make tender love to each other,
In all its beauty and grace,
Her slightly wet hair tickles him,
And he lets out a sigh,
Her flushed body against his own,
Curled up on the bed, they lie,
Oblivious to the existence of anyone else,
Gazing into each other's eyes,
The two bodies, unite into one soul,
Under the starry skies...

The Mermaid

The graceful mermaid swam,
In the clear blue sea,
He lay, carefree, on the sand,
Watching her admiringly...

His gaze fixed on her,
And then their eyes met,
Lost into each other's eyes,
They remained, till sunset...

As darkness took over them,
She dived back into the sea,
He still waited searching for her signs,
He just couldn't set himself free...

Finally, he turned, tired of searching,
And not finding her anywhere in sight,
In hope of meeting her again,
He stayed awake all night...

Next day, he ran to the sea,
And waited for her on the beach,
He knew she was somewhere under the water,
So close, yet, so out of reach...

His soul craved for her love,
Finally, he decided to dive,
He plunged deep into the water,
Not caring about whether he would survive...

He swam around looking for her,
The water flowing into his lungs, taking away his breath,
He was losing hope of finding her,
And going closer and closer to death...

"Probably, she doesn't even love me," he thought,
He couldn't bear the pain anymore,
He swam back and got a big shock,
There, she lay, lifeless, on the shore...

He swept her into his arms,
And dived back into the water,
Not being able to share life together,
He decided to share death with her...

Finally they met in heaven,
Separated by no boundary,
Entwined in each other's love,
They remained, till eternity!

I love you...

Come hold my hand, gaze into my eyes,
Let's go for a walk, under the starry skies,
Let's watch out of the window through the bars,
Look at the rustling leaves, count endless stars,
Let's dance on a tune, going on and on,
Let's be madly in love, till both of us are gone,
Let's run in the green meadows with a herd of sheep,
Let our love be divine, pure and like the ocean, deep,
Since the day you have knocked on my heart's door,
I love you, my love, more and even more!

The land of dreams...

Far, far away, in the land of dreams,
I meet you every night,
You are right there, no barriers in between,
No battles to fight,
Everything's alright...

No fear of what tomorrow holds,
No grudges from yesterday,
Just you and me, wild and free,
As we walk along the way,
It's like child's play...

No wonder, I don't want to wake up,
To reality, staring me in the face,
Here we are busy, trying to keep up,
In this rat race,
For love, where is the time and space?

And so I long all day,
For the silence of the night,
Holding on to my dreams, tight,
Where we are together, no questions asked,
Darkness, sometimes, is so much better than light!

My autumn love...

The autumn winds blow gently,
In my ears, they sing melodies,
Of the love that once was,
And the love that shall always be...

I sit alone, with no one near,
Holding onto each memory, dear,
The empty space on the rusty bench waiting,
For someone to wipe my autumn tears...

The autumn leaves crushing under my feet,
I walk along the lonely street,
Longing to hold your hand just once,
I think of you with each heartbeat...

Mildly drenched in autumn rain,
I say to myself, yet again,
Seasons shall come and seasons shall go,
But my autumn love for you shall remain!

Adios, my love...

It's time...
To let go of the memories,
That I held onto for so long,
And allow you to move on,
Towards brighter tomorrows...
And so...
I carry them, snugly resting in my arms,
To the graveyard,
I dig their grave with a heavy heart,
My tears, I hope, they'll keep them warm for a while,
I lay them in slowly and seal it up,
The grave is sealed now, the burial successful,
And I walk away with pain in my eyes,
The rains aren't far,
Soon lilies shall bloom,
And the gentle winds will carry your scent to me,
I promise, I'll surely pay them a visit then,
But for now, let our memories rest in bliss,
Adios, my love,
And peace be with you!

Karunam

(Poems of sorrow & pain)

The bird that couldn't fly!

The bird stood on the edge alone,
And shuddered at the thought,
Of flying away, without support,
What if he were to fall off?

He remembered what his peers had said,
"Your wings are too tiny, they cannot bear
Your weight, oh, poor dear,
You wouldn't last two seconds in the air!"

He turned around and looked at dad,
Surely he'd have something to say,
Daddy shrugged his shoulders, and said,
"Chum, I'm sorry, you need to find your own way!"

Tears welling up, he ran to mom,
She gave him a half-hearted nod,
With doubtful eyes, she let out a sigh,
And he could tell, she wasn't too proud...

He went up to bro, surely he would know,
But bro was too busy to hear,
And so birdie walked off, with a heavy heart,
Filled with insecurity and fear...

And little birdie stood alone on the edge,
And dared not, step off the ledge,
The poor little bird that couldn't fly,
How I wish you had let him try!

The snowman

The jolly snowman, he stands alone,
His undying smile hides the hardships he's borne,
The inhuman cold, the frigid bites,
The tiresome days, and the lonely nights,
He waits on, in the deadly breeze,
For the shining sun, and the lush trees,
And when spring strikes, he stands in wonder,
When all of a sudden, the earth starts shaking under,
He melts, his tears unseen, his unheard screams,
Down he flows away, right into the stream,
The poor snowman who makes everyone smile,
Life gives him no joy, not even for a while,
The poor snowman, who brooks those deadly stings,
Alas, he'll never know the warmth of spring...

Bleeding diamond...

I am the dazzling diamond everyone adores,
I am the object of everyone's desire,
I am precious and rare,
And so very difficult to acquire...

I am everyone's envy,
Be it pearls, jewels or beads,
I hold supreme power,
I can cut till you bleed!

Once upon a time, I lay,
Deformed, black and crude,
Nobody loved me back then,
And nobody understood...

I vowed to change myself one day,
I wanted to be loved by all,
And in the process of acquiring fame,
I forgot to answer my inner call

I left my beloved behind,
To rise and attain glory,
And here I am, desirable yet lonely,
With no one to complete my story...

And millions, gazillions love me today,
They only see me shine,
But nobody knows that my heart,
Still lies in that coal mine...

Listen...

Another day gone by, another night beckons,
Lying in bed, I am staring away,
So much in my mind to speak about,
Yet, I have nothing to say...

I like to get lost in chaotic crowds,
With unfamiliar faces who don't seem to care,
I feel great comfort in their indifference,
Because genuine concern is oh, so rare...

And God forbid, the days I do choose to talk,
Hoping for someone to understand,
Are the days I end up feeling even more lost,
Not knowing where I am going to land...

Another day gone by, another night beckons,
With a million thoughts whirring in my head,
I pick up the phone to make a call,
But I choose to put it back down instead!

Hiding those scars

Underneath these thick layers,
Of glee-filled eyes,
Are tears waiting to gush down,
Underneath the million lies,
I tell you, and myself,
Is the single unsaid truth,
That, I am scared,
Scared to tell you who I am,
To bare my scars,
And feel that distant pain,
Yet again,
But even more so,
Lest you can't bear to see,
Beneath the beauty, the ugly,
And walk away,
So here I am, covering myself up,
Building more walls,
That no one can ever break through!

Fall from grace...

Encash upon it, while you have the chance,
Opportunity strikes only once on your door,
Glory shall last a day or two,
Praise, maybe a bit more...

What stays though, is the struggle,
And the vicious tentacles of fate,
And long before you realise,
You end up biting the bait...

Illusions, then, cloud your vision,
You feel you deserve it all,
You imagine everyone's on your side,
Till you encounter that mighty fall...

You slog and give it all you can,
After all, it's for your kith and kin,
You don't care about losing a few battles,
For in their victories, lie your wins...

But, ouch, all of a sudden, the damage is done,
Before you know, a slap in your face,
Unexpected, unthought of, unbelievable,
There it comes, your fall from grace!

Silenced desires...

In the woven gossamers of my mind,
A myriad of desires, I nestle,
Struggling through paths unknown,
I muffle my soul, I wrestle...

Against my will, for the greater good,
I make amends with my wants,
But the devils of desire, don't leave me alone,
They appear in my dreams and haunt...

Wishes unfulfilled, my soul so parched,
Craving to quench itself with fulfilment's nectar,
It struggles within, entrapped in my body,
Trying to get away, running helter-skelter...

But reality bites, stings like a scorpion,
Demands the cruel sacrifice of my desires,
I walk around the pyre of my dreams,
And I myself set them on fire...

In the heavens of sanctity,
Waiting to be caressed, my desires rest,
As I lead this incomplete life,
Forlorn, lonely, bereft!

Hasyam

(Poems of laughter and joy)

Goofy

I am a fairly smart girl,
With just a bit of bad luck,
I try so hard to avoid silly situations,
But invariably, I just get stuck!

Sometimes I search everywhere for my glasses,
Only to find them on my head,
And sometimes I wake up, only to,
Find myself under my bed...

Sometimes I happen to walk,
Right into a glass wall,
And sometimes I am just walking,
And I end up having a fall...

Sometimes I am laughing so hard,
That I end up letting out a snort,
And sometimes I am trying to conceal a yawn,
And I happen to get caught!

Like I said, I am a smart girl,
Only with a goofy bent,
Who cannot really avoid silly situations,
All I can do, is vent!

Hallucination

Last night, I took a couple of puffs,
And as the smoke came out of my nose,
I suddenly felt all powerful,
Stood in front of the mirror and struck a pose...

"Wow, that's a really handsome lad,"
I said to myself, with a smirk,
I wore my superhero suit, put on my cape,
And set out, ready for work...

I walked the streets looking for trouble,
Thugs trying to loot a rich man,
I was prepared to save some damsel in distress,
Put my superhero powers to the best use that I can...

And then out of nowhere, my time came,
At the other end of the lane, was a mighty beast,
Threatening to kill a poor little boy,
I had to act fast so that he was seized...

I caught hold of the beast with my bare hands,
And dragged him away from the terrified chap,
I took off my cape and used it to tie him up,
And tamed him down with a couple of slaps

Today morning, I woke up on the street,
Only to realize, I was hallucinating all night,
There lay a tiny puppy, tied up to a rag,
Everyone's a superhero, after a few lights!

Fit as a fiddle!

Last week I decided,
To go on a diet,
So I have been eating,
Just one dinner per night!

Eating healthy is key,
That's what it takes,
So I have been adding lots of fruit,
To my chocolate cream cake!

And I have to admit,
I already feel light,
My necktie has stopped,
To feel all that tight!

I am supplementing my diet,
With some exercise as well,
I now actually answer the door,
When someone rings the bell!

It's difficult to get fit,
Is what people do say,
But let me tell you, for me,
This is just child's play!

Baby's the boss!

Adults think their lies are too smart,
For babies to be able to catch,
Mom, I know the magic formula you talked about,
Is just a spoonful of spinach...

And if the storks had, indeed,
Delivered my baby brother,
Don't you think I would have immediately,
Exchanged him for another?

I can see for myself, that my new tooth,
Is erupting from under my gum,
Yet you want me to go bury the fallen one,
And wait for the tooth fairy to come?

And if a simple kiss on a wound,
Was enough to make the pain go away,
Why are you popping pills after pills,
To get rid of that headache, anyway?

So the next time you lie to a baby,
And are silently praising yourself for your wit,
Remember, we could be pulling a fast one on you instead,
By pretending to believe it!

There's always a reason to smile!

Wandering in vain,
With the long-hidden pain,
You can't help but laugh out,
When you see jolly kids run about...

All alone on a cold night,
With not a soul in sight,
Helpless and shivering with fright,
Till you see that ray of light...

Getting drenched in untimely rain,
You think to yourself, "not again!"
Till suddenly a puddle comes your way,
And you jump into it and happily play...

When things have gone wrong all day long,
And you just can't figure out what went wrong,
Suddenly the phone rings, it's a long lost friend,
To your sorrows, he puts an end...

Through weary days and tough nights,
Through the long twisted path of life,
Sorrow does knock at your door once in a while,
But there's always a reason to smile!

Raudram

(Poems of anger & fury)

Infidel

He crept in, slowly, stealthily,
Put his arms around me,
And I knew, almost instantly,
That he was trying to confound me...

He held me firmly and whispered,
That he would never cheat,
And in that blatant lie,
Lay my very defeat...

For his shirt reeked of her scent,
Her texts filled his phone,
And he was lost in her eyes,
While I spent my nights alone...

Tears rolled down my cheek,
As I pushed him away,
My heart was screaming out loud,
But I had nothing to say...

And I walked out alone,
Caressing my bleeding heart,
That one unfortunate mistake of his,
Had torn all my dreams apart...

Granted, it's human to err,
But can someone please tell,
Is it even in God's capacity,
To forgive an infidel?!

Innocent Murderer...

Bloodstains everywhere,
I kill to win,
A ruthless human,
I err, I sin...

This thirst for success,
No one can quench,
But the smell of guilt,
Has an unbearable stench...

Still I continue to be cruel,
For the want of more,
I struggle to proceed,
And break all doors...

I have no compassion left,
For money and power, I strive,
Yes, I am a bloody human,
And I kill to survive!

Fake

I'd rather not smile,
If I can't smile with all my heart,
If I can't end it gracefully,
I wouldn't even care to start...

I simply can't pretend,
To like someone, I can't stand,
Isn't affection natural?
How the hell can it be planned?...

So, I would graciously accept,
All the hate you want to give,
But please don't pretend to like me,
It just makes it difficult to live...

For I truly believe that the truth,
Is much easier to take,
Than to have to deal,
With a world that is so fake!

I won't change

I shall stay the same,
You have no right to change me,
For there's more to me,
Than you really can see...

Go ahead and do what you want,
I don't give a damn,
Doesn't really matter to me,
Because I am, what I am...

I am good, I am great,
And I got the power, to shape my fate,
And if you have failed to understand me,
I feel really sorry for you, mate!

Broken, battered, smashed and shattered,
But still holding onto what is right,
I'll take the pain, but I won't change,
I shall stand tall and fight!

So, go torture someone else, buddy,
Because it's not going to work with me,
I will continue to fly, am a free spirit,
And shall remain one, eternally!

Taken for granted...

Don't come to me tomorrow,
With that empty hand stretched out,
Today I have a lot to give,
A lot more than you thought...

But who has seen tomorrow,
Life's as fickle as it can be,
And what the future holds,
No one in the world can see...

So take what I have today, to give,
And learn to appreciate,
And if you don't care enough now,
It might just be a bit too late...

For what's yours today,
Will be someone else's tomorrow,
And if you come asking for it later,
All life shall give you, is sorrow!

Bibhatsam

(Poems of disgust and disapproval)

Attacked Innocence...

Two young, innocent eyes,
With a tear dropping down from each one,
Stands the victim of a dirty man's lust,
Who used her just for his fun...

Thoughts haunt her mind,
Her innocence corrupted by his greed,
She knows the world out there is unkind,
Where contempt is sure to breed...

Helplessness engulfs her,
And the painful memories just don't seem to fade,
But all she can do is curse her culprit,
Who exposed her to life's grey shade!

"Will I ever get justice?"
Is the question that runs through her mind,
Is this really the world of God,
Where devils are all that she can find!

I can read her mind,
And she speaks through my words,
Both of us demand a change,
From those who have erred...

We hope no girl child goes through the same,
The trauma that she had to bear,
May this stimulate the warrior in each of you,
So that you stand up to fight, protect and care!

Ugly

Next time you flinch at the sight of someone's warty skin,
Or laugh at that stomach bulging out of someone's shirt,
Next time you wrinkle your nose and cover your mouth,
Around that rag-picker covered with slime and dirt,
Next time you turn your face away,
From the crippled beggar banging on your car door,
Next time you roll your eyes,
At the girl working as a whore,
Next time you shut your eyes,
When you see a man kissing another,
Next time you judge somebody for,
Their appearance, their character, their colour,
You may pity them for being ugly,
And you may be basking in your pride,
But look into the mirror of your own mind,
It's you who is really ugly on the inside!

Ignore the drama! Period.

No, there's no need to wipe that red stain,
Or feel shame over it,
As it is, you bravely hide your pain,
When you just aren't feeling fit...

Go on, feel free to touch,
The furniture, and the sheets,
And the pickle bottle too,
Indulge yourself, with a treat...

Sit on the table and eat,
In fact, you must eat really well,
The people who mind sitting next to you,
Can simply just go to hell...

And what else do they say?
Don't go anywhere near God,
Isn't God residing everywhere?
Which boundaries are they talking about?!...

You need to neither be worshipped nor punished,
You do not require to be treated differently,
Don't listen to these people telling you to 'behave'
You are as 'normal' and 'pure' as one can be!

A Man's World

Don't sit like that, girl,
With your legs spread out wide,
You are just trying to entice men,
By exposing your raw hide...

And don't talk too loudly, mind you,
Women aren't supposed to speak,
Their mind, unless asked for an opinion,
The chances of which are bleak...

Don't step out of the house after sunset,
Don't walk alone on the streets,
Don't mess with the heads of men,
And make them act like beasts...

And did you say you want to,
Work after marriage, No way!
Women were born to raise children,
And take care of the house all day...

This is a man's world, woman,
Where you have but a few rights,
And if you want to live life on your terms,
Then darling, come join the fight!

Sad & Gay

I was born, like everybody else,
I looked like any other baby boy,
My mom's warm hands comforting me,
And my dad pampering me with toys...

I went to school, bright-eyed, each day,
I was a good student, teachers would say,
Loving friends, doting parents, life was perfect,
Till I realised that I was gay...

Girls like boys, and boys like girls,
Then why do I not feel that way,
If God is impartial and makes everyone the same,
How, then, did I turn out to be gay?

I do realise that I am different,
But am I so different, really?
Why is it that me being gay,
Is the only trait that people can see...

I fear stepping out in the crowd,
People look at me in a disdainful way,
I am scared to speak out, the things I want to say,
Do I have no right to live, just because I am gay?

I always thought, loving unconditionally,
Is all that matters at the end of the day,
I never knew love had to wear
Tags like straight, lesbian and gay...

I hide my feelings in a box,
I don't want my friends to go away,
I don't want my parents to disown me,
Please don't tell them, I am gay...

I crave to be like everyone else,
For a normal life, I constantly pray,
For a day, when people won't discriminate,
And I can say with pride, that I am gay!

Am I safe, Mumma?!

I was walking to school today,
And my classmate lifted my skirt,
I complained to the teacher, she said,
First, properly button up your shirt...

Uncle came over the other day,
Asked me to come sit on his lap,
And immediately put his hand,
Between my legs, in the gap...

I don't like going to the babysitter,
Though she lets me watch TV,
Because men and women without clothes,
Is all that she makes me see...

Just yesterday, I got into the bus,
A grandpa was sitting next to me,
I simply don't understand why his elbow,
Kept hitting me continuously...

Mumma, you told me I am a strong girl,
I swear, I am trying to be brave,
But when everyone's out to exploit me,
How do I possibly feel safe?!

Bhayanakam

(Poems of fear & terror)

Schizophrenic

People say you don't exist,
But stranger you haunt my soul,
You creep inside slowly,
When the deep dark night falls...

You light that tremendous fire,
Which warms me deep inside,
And whisper slowly into my ears,
And then just go and hide...

You make my body tremble,
And crave to be with you,
And I keep searching all night,
Till I see the morning's hue...

I sigh, I cry, I mourn,
One more night without your touch,
Oh stranger, tell me why,
Why do I want you so much?

People say I am crazy,
But I know you'll be mine someday,
I am no schizophrenic,
Or whatever else they say!

The devil is born

My faith put to test,
My heart beats no more,
I sleep in unrest,
As sorrow knocks on my door,
I know no comfort,
I know of no joy,
Each part of me hurts,
This pain, I want to destroy,
I wake up to a world of misery,
To a world of mistrust,
I am fed up of other's treachery,
And my feelings just lie and rust...

And now my blood boils,
I feel different, I feel strange,
My inner self toils,
Now, I seek revenge,
I no longer feel weary,
I feel powerful, I feel strong,
I grow ugly, I grow scary,
To a different genre, now I belong,
Conceived in moments of distress,
From emotions shattered and torn,
From the womb of helplessness,
Now, the devil is born!

My nemesis

I wake up every morning with bruises all over,
Too tired to walk, too numb to feel,
Blood oozing from inhuman wounds,
And the floor covered in bits of torn hair,
I crawl slowly, pull out the drawer,
Clean the wounds, dress them all up,
Wipe off the bloodstains, destroying evidence,
Of the gruesome event that got me to this state,
I lie down, tired, trying to remember how it happened,
And fall asleep soon, like I would never wake up,
And then I rise, bring out the weapons,
Pull out my own skin, exposing the flesh,
Breaking myself down, part by part,
Finally, exhausted, I slip into a deep slumber,
Only to wake up oblivious to the truth,
That I am, my own nemesis,
And that, I would never know!

It's always dark in here...

The signs often foretell,
What's in store, in a place like this,
Far away it rings, the suspicion bell,
It tells you, something's amiss...

Screams echo through the hallways,
Telling you to stay away,
And you know it's serious business,
This ain't no child's play...

Yet you keep inching closer and closer,
To the place where danger looms,
And you keep moving on bravely,
Through dingy passageways and rooms...

And finally, you reach a point,
From where there's no turning back,
Frantically searching for some light,
For some colour, in the pitch black...

Few dare to enter a swarthy heart,
But those who do seldom return,
You are one of those unfortunate souls,
And what's done, can't get undone...

You've come too far now,
So, say hello to your worst fears,
Welcome to my world, stranger,
It's always dark in here!

The shadow in the dark...

Creeping up stealthily,
That shadow in the dark,
Muffled footsteps kill the silence,
The contrast, so stark...

The air, still, no more,
Screeching winds start to blow,
My heartbeats rise and sink,
As fears start to grow...

He walks slowly towards me,
Surprisingly unarmed,
And I think to myself
He can do me no harm...

For he seems so fragile,
I almost instantly pity his state,
Not once do I doubt,
That his appearance could be a bait...

I raise my hand to ward him off,
He retraces, taken aback,
I tighten my fists, point them at him,
I can hear my knuckles crack...

Suddenly he starts moving towards me,
His grimness changes to a malicious grin.
And instantly, a shiver runs down my spine,
His confidence makes my head spin...

A gust of wind appears from nowhere,
The window panes start to creak,
And through his firmly clenched teeth,
He slowly and carefully speaks...

"Oh, ignorant fool, so full of yourself,
Have you no sense, don't you know,
And didn't it ever occur to you,
That it takes light, to form a shadow!"

The Pit

I didn't quite realise,
When I entered the pit,
Or when the base kept shifting,
Pulling me in deeper into it...

I did fight a bit initially,
Survival instinct, probably,
And while I struggled to breathe at first,
Soon I started living quite normally...

The pit is a strange place,
Alien, yet somehow, familiar,
You develop comfort in here,
Yet somewhere there is a constant fear...

Minutes, hours keep ticking by,
As I live on, in this dingy pit,
The problem is not the darkness, really,
The problem is that I am getting used to it!

Veeram

(Poems of courage & heroism)

The flag on the hill...

The storm is raging,
Dark is the sky,
The flag flutters alone on the hill,
Struggling to stay up high...

Life seems to me like this flag,
It takes you to a certain height,
And to stay high up there,
You have to put up a big fight...

All your life you strive,
To go up there,
And then the burden of victory,
Seems difficult to bear...

With success comes responsibility,
Both go hand in hand,
And you've to learn to stand tall,
Wherever you may land...

You have to face all struggle,
And bear all pain and ill,
If you wish to survive,
Like the flag on the hill!

Failure – The biggest inspiration

It's only when things go wrong,
That we try to set them right,
Only when life pulls us down,
Do we put up a big fight,
Only when we fall down,
We struggle to reach new heights,
And only after darkness,
Does the world appear bright!

There's no joy without trouble,
No achievement without struggle,
No pleasure without pain,
And no sunshine without rain,
No laughter without tears,
No bravery without fear,
No rose without thorns,
And without dusk, no dawn!

Sorrow gives us strength,
And misery gives rise to desire,
When life turns all blue,
Hope is what ignites the fire,
Smooth roads are no fun,
For obstacles give determination,
Defeat is what pushes us towards victory,
Failure is, but the biggest inspiration!

Consequences

I always wonder why,
People take so much time to choose,
Contemplating what one would gain,
And what one would lose...

For, how are we to decide,
Where our choices shall lead?
All we can do is accept,
The consequences of our deeds...

So why fret about our choices,
Why not just give our best?
Instead of cowering in fear,
Gear up to face the test...

Why spend sleepless nights worrying,
Whether what we chose is right?
Nobody ever cares about the path taken,
As long as the result is bright...

Choices don't make a man what he is,
Facing the consequences does,
And if we strive to face the consequences,
There sure would be a hero within each of us!

The rock by the sea

The waves lash, they lash hard at me,
Yes, I am the rock, that stands by the sea...

Long ago, I was, like any other stone,
Rolling along, the path that was shown...

Slipping away, I never cared too much,
There really wasn't anything, to worry about as such...

Till I landed one day, next to the ocean vast,
In the wall next to it, I was cast...

And all of a sudden, I had to bear the brunt,
Of the many waves, that were, oh, so blunt...

They struck me hard, made me whine and cry,
But I didn't give up, I stood high...

And slowly I realised, my rough edges were no more,
The waves were smoothening me, every time they hit the shore...

The pain that I had borne made me stronger each day,
I am no longer an ordinary rock, by the way...

Here I am, the rock by the sea,
Smooth and glistening, in all my glory!

Courage

To bear a bullet,
Is painful for sure,
But to bear piercing words,
Which have no cure,
And yet keep smiling,
With your head held high,
Is the kind of courage,
That's hard to come by!

Courage doesn't always roar,
It could be silent determination,
It is the tolerance to bear more,
And the will to still get things done,
It just isn't about outwardly brawn,
It is about inward strength,
Holding onto dreams, come what may,
And to be ready to go to any length!

True courage is to accept defeat,
And get ready for the next fight,
Smile in the face of misery,
Even when nothing is going right,
True courage is not about winning,
It is about losing with grace,
It is about not running away,
Even when failure stares you in the face!

But she believed

Just like that,
Based on a whim,
They took away,
Almost everything,
That she had built,
With so much care,
Her heart ached,
She knew it wasn't fair,
But she believed...

So she fought with all her might,
Turned every stone,
When fate turned its back on her,
She still stood tall, alone,
She didn't give in,
To empty threats,
She was committed to try,
Till her last breath,
Because she believed...

And despite her tries,
When people believed lies,
Didn't give her a chance to speak,
It all looked very bleak,
She knew in her heart,
That this battle's not hers to win,
But she is prepared for the big war,
She won't just give in,
Because she believes!

Adbhutam

(Poems of surprise and wonder)

Raindrops

The raindrops trickle down on me,
They have their own story to tell,
They strum at the strings of my heart,
And make a new story dwell...

To some, rain brings pain,
To some, it brings joy,
For some, it's a reason to celebrate,
For some, a shelter to cry...

But for me, rain brings hope,
Of new dreams, new beginnings,
Washing away the painful past,
And wiping my slate clean...

And as I sit down to write my story,
The raindrops trickle down on me,
Clearing away all the dust,
Creating a clean tomorrow for me to see!

Dream On!

When the tired and weary mind,
Retires for the day,
It, ironically, weaves thoughts,
Adding imagination along the way...

In this enchanting world of dreams,
Mysteries unravel, unfold,
Each night you tell yourself,
A story that's never been told...

In a land of endless possibilities,
Filled with colours and charms,
You create magical situations,
Some shake you up, while some calm...

You never know what to expect,
Nor can you control what you see,
This land of dreams is indeed,
The most enthralling place to be!

Anything can happen in this place,
So tonight, lay in your blanket, rolled,
Close your eyes, paint your canvas,
Discover a new surprise, lo and behold!

My moment of bliss...

The cool breeze blowing through my hair,
I lie, wondering, in my chair,
The enchanting smell of rain-soaked earth,
The tiny birds joining in my mirth,
I smile to myself, enjoying the moment,
The sweet air with its beautiful scent,
Everything looks so miraculous around,
Like heaven on earth, I have found,
Everything's perfect today, nothing's amiss,
The perfect moment, my moment of bliss!

Green

Dear green, sprightly and fresh,
I am so in love with you,
Sparkling, resplendent,
With tiny pearls of dew...

Gently swaying, caressed by the wind,
Humming your own sweet song,
Green is all I want to see,
Can I please take you along?

I wonder why they tag you as envy,
Fail to notice your beauty, pristine,
Oh, if only the world was my canvas,
I would paint it all green...

You spell love, in all its purity,
No red, white, yellow, blue can take your place,
Oh, when he smiles at me,
I just want to splash some green on his face...

Dear green, where are you disappearing?
It saddens my heart that you've become so rare,
I wish I could just bottle you up,
And sprinkle green magic, everywhere...

For won't the world be a better place,
With you, dear green, adorning Mother Earth?
No wonder, the world, is devoid of joy,
Oh green, how I wish, people realised your worth!

Shantham

(Poems of peace, tranquillity & hope)

Solitude

In the crowd,
I forget myself,
I never knew,
Till I met myself,
In solitude...

It is so nice,
To get to know,
Who I am,
Nice and slow,
In solitude...

At peace,
I feel,
All my wounds,
Slowly heal,
In solitude...

My worry creases,
Relax, unfold,
As I narrate to myself,
All the stories untold,
In solitude...

I have not a care,
My lips break into a smile,
And I say to myself,
Hope this stays for a while,
This solitude...

We always want more people around,
To quench our endless greed,
But sometimes, to come to terms with life,
All we really need,
Is solitude!

A sound mind

For money, fame, power,
We crave, we slave,
We fight constantly,
Till we lie in our graves...

We trample upon many,
To gain advantage, to lead,
The crop of success is often sown,
With polluted and corrupt seeds...

Oh, what a price we pay,
We sell our souls to win,
And spend sleepless nights,
To pay for our sins...

Riches are easy to obtain,
Peace, most difficult to find,
Of all the riches on earth,
The best is a sound mind!

Let today be no exception

Each morning as the sun rises high,
My dreams, my aspirations, touch the sky,
Let today be no exception...

Each day I am put to test,
And I gear up to give my best,
Let today be no exception...

Each day I struggle to proceed,
To move forward and take the lead,
Let today be no exception...

Each day there's something new to do,
And each day I learn a lesson new,
Let today be no exception...

Each day I laugh a little more,
And each day I cry a little more,
Let today be no exception...

As each day knocks upon life's door,
It teaches me to love a little more,
Let today be no exception...

Each day of life is a new gift,
For us to enjoy before it drifts,
Let today be no exception!

Renew

The demanding world says whiling time's a sin,
But with worries aplenty, reliefs but a few,
Don't shy away from looking within,
Cleanse your soul, renew...

The music of life isn't only about beats,
And the high notes that attract the crowd,
In the low notes are hidden, many treats,
The best moments of life are seldom spoken aloud...

Who but me knows 'me' so well,
And has stood by me, through rise and fall,
The face in the mirror has many stories to tell,
And yet you choose to ignore its faint call...

Listen to the melody, carefully,
Let it not get muffled in the cacophony around,
Resting in sanctity, blissfully,
You shall discover the truths of life, unfound!

The Pursuit Of Happiness...

The pursuit of happiness,
It starts with a dream,
The more you try to move closer to it,
The more elusive it seems...

You share your dream with others,
Hoping they'd empathize,
But all they do is create doubts in your head,
And self-doubt is but, the biggest vice...

And more often than not,
These doubts will pull you down,
Let not your spirit dwindle,
Just keep racing on...

Protect your dream fiercely,
Work towards it, achieve,
If you fail, don't lose heart,
And when you feel lost, believe...

For if you believe in them,
Dreams do come true,
The pursuit of happiness,
It ends at 'you'!

Why hate mediocrity???

What is it about mediocrity,
That people so despise?
The way I see it, it gives you,
An eternal opportunity to rise!

Stuck in the middle somewhere,
There's always a burning desire to win,
All the same, you have the humility to give up,
But never to give in!

And you know your place, you are secure,
In the midst of brilliant and poor,
And since you can go either way,
You work harder to be sure...

You neither have the greed for victory,
Nor, the fear of loss,
For somehow, you've seen both sides of the coin,
Both, heads and tails, of a toss...

So don't hate being mediocre,
Because it gives you no reason to regret,
Mediocrity is a boon, it gives you a choice,
That others, often, do not get!

About the Author

Mona Aiyar is a human resources management professional by day, and a poet by night. At the tender age of 7, Mona discovered the joy of rhyming and expressing her emotions through poetry. Since then, she has penned hundreds of poems - some published in magazines, others on her blogs and social media handles. Her readers often appreciate her poetry for being lucid, relatable, moving and carrying a powerful message. Mona lives in Mumbai with her family. In her free time, she loves to cook, travel, and dance.

You can connect with Mona on her Instagram handle @monaaiyar or mail her on monaaiyar@gmail.com.